"Daddy, in the elevation, in the vibration of light intertwined, we blend in the river of electric water that warmly pulses its current in a steady flow from God's own heart." - Kayleigh

Pre-Script Murmur.

You are sitting with me in a cloud white top and your Exuma turquoise blue shorts. Your long golden blonde hair, it shines like a warm, blinding sunrise. Your deep blue eyes are oceans of light. Your smile, the universe. You are here. Spiritually. Yet physically, with torture, you have been ripped from my arms.

We have stamped some of these moments into the mystic wind of our Jekyll Island, in the humid electricity of a powerful Georgian beachfront breeze. Spirits live here, in this holy, spiritual garden of grace and elevation. We have always known and felt this, even before your innocent accident that stripped you, robbed you of your physical life; transitioned you into your higher life. This is the sacred ground of guardian angels, blending light and love and enlightenment into a tapestry of interconnection, particularly with loved ones still in the finite journey of human life.

Before the accident, we would talk about this interconnection, where the dimensions crisscross, where God's bridge of love permits, facilitates, encourages these connections. I do vividly recall nights in the darkness on our dunes at our beachfront home, 10 Austin Lane, your brother hanging out in his bedroom, my time with him also sure to come and be just as vibrant; your mother relaxing slumped and relaxed on the couch with a book. Yet you and I, we the lovers of the outdoors, electrified by the haunts of the night, and of this beach, and of the galaxy pinwheels; if not walking with the sea turtles or shark fishing in the darkness, would be found on our beach under the shooting stars, a Daddy and his Daughter, so engaged, effortlessly, so in love with each other, teaching each other, growing endlessly with each other, sitting in silence or laughing uncontrollably. Usually laughing. Okay, almost always laughing. Our laughter is alive in the stitching of the wind for all eternity.

Then, out of nowhere, at fifteen years old, the accident happened, Kayleigh, and you were horrifically physically killed against your will in a pedestrian car accident you did not cause while taking care of yourself and trying to cross the street to go for a walk with your mother, transitioning in my arms four minutes after you were struck.

Time tortures me, as each day takes me further and further away from the last time I physically held you. My sweet and funny Kayleigh, living a dynamic, happy incredible life, higher and more profoundly than anyone I have ever known. Pure brilliance.

I am in the middle of this every second of every day with incredible warrior courage as time opens this wound larger by the day. Time terribly takes me away further each day from the last time I held you, my daughter, physically. No, time is a thief and a thief only, the accumulator of daily losses. In the midst of that, God is present with us four with extreme love and light.

The essence of pure hell is being forced to be physically without you, Kayleigh, for one day. By simple math we lose 10 interactions a day with you and those physical losses accumulate over time (laughter, meals, texts, time together, hikes, walks, vacations, leaving for school, watching tv, etc.). At day 10 it was 100. On day 100 it was 1,000. On day 1,000 it was 10,000. Now, living this one day at a time, that hell has stretched over 2,300 days and 23,000 physical losses, and growing. That is the physical death of a child in full color and its full magnitude. To not acknowledge the fullness of those physical losses is to deny, disrespect and minimize you, Kayleigh, and I refuse to do that. I know some others don't like facing this daily harsh truth, but this is the brutality of the physical death of a child, which in courageously facing, opens me further to your daily presence.

Since day 1, Kayleigh, we together learned how to counter these physical losses with our ongoing relationship, physical to spiritual, doing 10 spiritual intentional things a day together. I am beyond blessed that you, Kayleigh, in your Higher Life are here with me in profound ways. We countered these 2,300 days so far with 23,000 spiritual gains. We have attempted to balance this unimaginable grief with incredible presence and have succeeded on this road thus far. I know the disbelief, the eye rolling of some, the hurtful shunning, as if they somehow know our story better in their failure in faith, when we intimately take the risk to tell them that literally, you are alive in your Higher Life, active, present, and growing with us. Those voices do not matter. They will sadly disbelieve what they disbelieve. Our tears and our laughter together tell another tail in this duality. I love you, my brilliant daughter, and am increasingly more and more proud of all that we do to grow in strength together daily.

The duality is upon us, forcing us to learn new ways of building our relationship. We have been magnificent together, transitioning our relationship just as your life was transitioned from the shell of your physical body to the enlightenment of your spirit body. The same old kid, just elevated one thousand fold. The counterbalance strings the miracle beads that make up the chain of life we wear and share around our necks and hang down on our chests. We pass these beads we each fill with our love for each other in the activities we pick for us for each day. Those are the most sacred of quiet moments, where we grow, where we breathe this truth.

Then there are the other moments, the counter to the counterbalance. Shattered lungs, burning throat from the ungodly depth and volume attained in the shriek explosively; it exhausts my entire frame, puffing up and down in convulsive shoulder strain as my voice collapses to a whisper and whimper in the desolate darkness of complete powerlessness. It is five shades darker than the perfect darkness under a moonless night. No hummingbirds vibrate the air. These releases contain the most indescribable, grotesque screeching death screams that only emanate from a parent in an overwhelmed moment of complete frustrating suffering; grieving endlessly and hopefully for and to a child who has physically died.

It is then, that worst form of powerlessness, that the salt wind draped darkness of the south end of Jekyll Island opens its mouth and offers our entrance. And into its velvety throat we walk.

SOUNDS NO HUMAN SHOULD MAKE

"Sounds No Human Should Make"

A banshee bewildered caught screaming in my throat,
Wearing barbed wire thread and fire blades as its overcoat,
Shredding the lining of the esophageal membrane,
And spinning incessantly like erratic hurricane,
Until the wind is spent,
And the damage is deeply done,
The sounds no human should make,
Are made in these moments…

…When the mounting pressure breaks;

In a place that sees no sun,
In a face that sets no sun,
In a trace of pure and raging tears,
Not only for the pain logged to date,
But also for the coming years,
The sounds no human should make,
And made in these moments…

…When the anguish is so heavy,
From the incessant pressure,
That the soul itself breaks.

"Daddy, how awful that sounds and how grateful I am to hear you release its pitch. There were no other cars near the water tower. We are alone here. Let it out, Father. I am so proud of you and I love you so much. Let's walk. There are some turtle mothers out there waiting for us. Will you find a Loggerhead with me and watch her lay her eggs with me, just like we would always do? Will you?"

"The Temple Of The Soul"

The darkness, it is so dark,
The emptiness, so empty full,
When the waves rush over the mountains,
And explode into the valley road,
Scarring the landscape,
Where once the life was plentiful,
A lunar surface remains in its wake,
A debris field of anguish exhales in the lull,
Before the darkness darkens further,
And the emptiness overflows,
I stand here irreparably stunned,
Awaiting the next wave of grief,
To pound into dust…

…The temple of the soul.

"Starfish In Tidal Pools"

Yet, among the drapes of stinging heartache,
Akin to sacred presence,
Little souls of silence stir in oblong puddles,
And stranded low tide pools,
Blanketed in cloaks of bioluminescence,
These tidal pools, the perfect temperature of love,
Quietly clinging to the nutrient rich bottom,
Awaiting the turn of the tide,
Where they camouflage as they can,
Yet give off a florescent green sign,
Five tiny legs,
Starfish in the tidal waters,
Hide…

…The lore of vibration is strong in these spirits,
The door of spirituality their domain.

"Drowning In A Wave Of Grief"

i.   I Drown

Imagine,
Drowned with the suffocating tension of my own tears,
Flowing inward behind the eyes,
And downward with heavy unseen cries,
Catching in an inescapable chamber,
Over-flooding in the over emergence,
Each day the catch calls me on the rise,
Regardless of emotional deterrence,
For the spirit and it's lungs,
Have been long overloaded and succumbed,
With these overwhelming streams,
These tears…

…In which I drown;

ii.   These Tears

Sometimes these tears slide down the inside of my eyes,
Down the inside of my body,
And pool in my stomach,
Lacerating my spirit with an abysmal pain,
And sometimes these tears are evident to the masses,
Visible and flowing outward,
Where, on my face, they leave their stain,
And sometimes these tears,
These tears,
These tears…

…They are all that is left of me.

"A Bed Of Grief"

So deeply I am thread into this sheath,
Imbedded in a bed of grief;

So deeply am I webbed twined like a rusted red wreath,
Bedded down in a bed of grief;

So kept from me I dreamt of sleep,
While sleeping in this bed of grief;

I wept enough to fill an ancient sea,
Deadened in this empty bed of grief.

"The Sound Of This Type Of Parent Crying"

So loud are these guttural screams, the uninvited may hear from a distant beach chair sitting alone aloofly in the dunes off in the darkness; a banshee; a bobcat; a human being shedding impossibly insufferable layers of spectral colors of severe sadness; maybe they think a racoon has just been shredded and murdered by an alligator; maybe they think nothing at all;

The oak trees absorb the vibration;

In the other distance two lovers hear this echoing yet faint sound in the wind, and empathetically pause; starfish in the tidal pools shudder and tighten up as the water vibrates; ghost crabs scurry and retire to their labyrinth sensing the uneasy and sudden danger in the air; yet the turtles, the turtles continue wisely on their journey in the darkness, knowing the sound of this type of parent crying, solemnly stopping to absorb the vibration and bow their beaks into the sand to the sound in holy prayer.

Convulsive Grief"

i. Heavier Daily

Flicker and flake,
Sleepless awake,
Dust breathes from the seams,
And the circling glaze,
That blurred the vision for days,
Lies glistening, blanket dreams…

…Watching closely the sands of time collect,
Accumulate in weight and sorrowful effect…

…Heavier, daily, it seems;

ii. Grieving My Child

Bound in each breath…

…And man for his bedevilments,
A locust swarm for this dream,
A biblical absorption of menacing chains,
Pinch off the rifled catacombs of the veins,
And exhaust like pulverized, pressurized, escaping steam,
Through the coils of overheating screams,
That grind down the human engine,
As the pistons melt into the flesh…

…Of the worst grain of human pain.

"Time"

Time it tolls larger from the last time I held you,
Time it grows in its chasm and stain,
Time it flows further away day by day,
Accumulating daily the diary of a much deeper pain;

For time does not heal all wounds,
For this wound is one that remains,
For time makes the grief much steeper,
To crawl out of each new day;

And time it just takes me further away,
From the last time I held you, My Love,
Time just makes this worse over time,
Harder and heavier…

…Day after day after day…

"The Huntsman"

A torch animates scurrying shadows in the woods,
Flitter flickering fire,
And fan the flames of solvency,
In the quickening pace of the spreading mire,
For the backroads lead away,
From the dangers of the day,
Sometimes rather than facing it directly,
It is prudent to go another way,
And flank the horror with a gentle tongue,
Or shank the beast before its claws are sprung,
Whatever the case and whatever the desire,
Flitter on this flickering fire,
For the hunting has begun.

"Pages Within Pages"

An insufferable sobbing,
A weeping for the ages,
Yet it happens every morning,
Locked into cages within cages,
I scream for my baby,
I dig in my heels to prevent possible falter,
And punch a hole through the universe,
To stand beside my beautiful daughter,
Like a warrior in our fables,
A thousand deaths I would suffer through,
Just to hold your spirit's hand,
Just to stand beside you,
And so I suffer through insufferable sobbing,
And weep through the cracks in these cages,
And bleed my soul in fractious splinters,
Across these pages within pages within pages.

"Inch By Inch"

Crying through the pores of my skin,
While societal impressed smile lines my face,
Screaming, the tears eviscerate,
And damage the temples I have built,
The holy landscape within,
Wailing, the crevasses, the corridors vibrate,
As the spirit's resolve wears thin,
Crying through the swollen pores,
I crawl forward inch by inch,
Along this sacred coastal shore,
Through plaster flakes and buckling floors,
On knees that momentum cannot refuse,
On knees deep punctured and infused…

…With shards of shells like needles and pins.

"Daddy, remember we used to say, the one who is processing feelings is not the one for which worry should seek? You are processing with me these torturous feelings, these terrible troubles that come from my physical absence. That is so smart! Scream, Daddy, scream. Who cares if anybody hears you. We are out here on our beach. The angels are your audience, and the trees, and a loggerhead down the beach in the darkness, and the bobcats. And Me! Daddy, I am right here. Keep walking."

"The Mathematics Of The Physical Death Of A Child"

It does not heal. It gets worse over time. Time does two things - takes me further and further away from the last time I held my baby, and, it also accumulates day after day each day's terrible grief. With the physical death of a child the death is backwards in time; unnatural in its order. The parent, now backward in time to their own death, lives each day as they would not have, not getting the chance to watch their child grow up and experience life until that parent died with their children looking on.

To give an example, I lose 10 things a day. Each day this happens. Texts. Lunches. Phone conversations. Sitting on the couch. Laughing. Crying. Planning life. Life's events. All of it. After 10 days I lost 100 moments. At 100 days I lost 1,000 moments. At 1,000 days I had accumulated 10,000 losses. And on until I physically die. We are not making grief. We are not failing to face grief. We are actually courageously facing the worst thing a human can face and acknowledging that the losses are constant and will be for the rest of my life. There is no way around that even if one tries to put it in the past, whatever that means.

When survivors claim to heal, they could be inadvertently treating the passing of a child as an event in time, to which healing can be applied, which it is not. It is a daily, longitudinal continuance from that initial inception of this nightmare until the physical death of the increasingly heartbroken parent. The target, instead, should be daily reconciliation, applying the right ointment, the tool of daily spiritual reconciliation, which allows for a counterbalance each day to the torture of daily physical absence.

"While I Sleep"

While I sleep…

…A mystic visitation,
A vindictive vindication,
A ministry, a needed vacation,
From the weight of this grief,
Come walk with me, my child,
Mile after angel mile,
Laughing together,
While I sleep;

While I sleep…

…The defenses weaken,
And I awaken,
While I sleep,
A fertile ground for advancement,
Yard by yard is taken,
While I sleep,
In each vision that you give me to breathe,
While I feel you,
While I hear you,
While I see you…

…While I sleep.

"Without A Warning"

And lower vibration it rise in the hollow,
And lowered vibration flags a gasping, fleeting tongue;

Waves in waves will naturally rise,
But there is no rhythm you will find,
As natural are waves on the ocean of grief,
As waves on the sea are undefined,
Until they crash and batter and thieve,
And shock and torture and grind,
And as you feel it hard to breathe,
And unprepared again this time,
Blame not oneself against this foe…

…That comes without a warning sign.

"A Longing In The Memory Of Christmas Chess"

In the corner of the living room,
Where rise the scent of pine and cinnamon perfume,
Lapping with lights that claimed the candles,
Blazing above us while we sit under the mantle,
Braving intellect and amusing releases,
Shuffling indigo and pearly white chess pieces,
Across a board of checkered glass that illuminates,
The reflection of your beautiful face;

Laughter fills the room while your brother plays,
Video games on the couch just feet away,
And Mommy with her delicate eyes feeds the cats,
A woman worn of many hats,
She leans over and whispers moves to you,
As I joke repercussions if you follow through,
Watching the corners of your lips rise,
A smile as big as your beautiful eyes,
Trapping your father's bishop in the corner,
On a night of Christmas chess…

…What I now would give for one moment,
Millions of these in which our souls invest,
What I now would give for that physical closeness,
In my shriek is found the truth I confess,
What I would give for that moment now…

…Everything…

…Everything.

"Empty Worship"

Patterned in the lurking shock of stalking intrusions,
Staring out over the horizon's gurgling gray curve,
Of disillusion,
Comes arching toward the penultimate regression,
A banshee logged in the nodes of the throat,
Dressed up in barbed wire fishhook overcoat,
The psychology of assumption kicking alive,
How chiefly wane ignored,
So deeply gnawed in swampy marrow,
That the wrong bone is explored,
My confidence has receded like the sun swallowed by a storm,
Yet it remains, obscured as it may appear to disappear,
No vanishing in lack of vision,
Baptized in the church of spiraling derision,
I pause –

Choosing a particular path and absorbing its opulence,
Or its inherent flurry of unintended consequences,
Bend against your reluctance,
Lean into that which you fear,
Envy worship in empties eyes,
Until the fullness of emptiness disappears,
Until the vacancy is filled with prayers,
So dedicated in the delicate recital of tears.

"Each Hour The Hammer Falls"

In the fields of Exuma Infinite,
Graced with layers of crystal waves,
They roll, they shift, they laugh and tumble,
They set a smile on the beach's sandy face,
When I am partly in Exuma Infinite,
Then I am partly able to embrace,
The terrible challenge upon me,
This terrible torturous weight;

I am the expert architect of my life,
For no one knows my life like me,
I am the narrator of the road ahead,
I am the cartographer,
Carefully translating the ocean's ebbs,
Flowing in the current,
And managing the grief with purposeful intent,
Speak not loose words lacking wisdom,
Speak little if you must at all,
For ears of wisdom are what we need,
Each hour the hammer falls.

"There Is No Nothing"

If nothing breathe the air,
If nothing was or wasn't here,
If nothing then beware;

If nothing worried you,
If nothing bothered you,
If nothing - do you care;

If nothing challenged you,
If nothing balanced you,
If nothing - what is truth;

If nothing to pursue,
If nothing we can do…

…Then nothing we will do.

"Tied To A Dark Quiet Dock"

 i.   *A Wet Rope*

A wet rope wrapped in knots squeaks in the void,
Rubbing against mooring as the trickling waters flow,
Rocking, a skiff pitches slightly stretching this rope,
That speaks of the grueling tension,
That only a lonely dock may know;

 ii.   *Open Water Road*

A skiff untended, a sail untold,
The material creased by years in its fold,
A main sheet moss moistened in the cupboard cold,
A blistered keel aching as it rocks afloat,
Not used for what it is built for,
The open water road;

 iii.   *Me*

If ever a loneliness deeper existed,
Than an empty skiff on a waveless sea,
If ever there was a more isolating feeling,
Than the slow drifting through sluggish misery,
Then this scene has come,
This scene has found central within it…

…Me;

If ever the parched aqua paint peeled to raw brown wood,
And the yellowed oaken grains chipped and bled into the sea,
Eroding the hull in the salty stillness,
Until this tiny flotsam ceases to be,

Then this scene will be welcome,
For mercy sinking is relief,
For a tiny skiff that had such promise,
For a crossing it once promised…

…Me;

    iv.   *Harbor Winds*

And in my hand now the presence of a frayed, soggy rope,
Yet still, hard jagged edges give me hope,
If only I can find the motivation,
To loosen from the dock post its incessant hold,
And I remember, and I know,
When the dare to dream was bold,
Before the trauma like a midnight robber,
Rifled through the safety of our spirit home,
Yet its promise is not now farther,
For our miracles, daily they have grown,
This skiff was built to leave the harbor,
The harbor of my soul,
And so,
And so…

…Back into the fray I go,
Back into the fray I go,
Back into the fray I go.

"Night Clouds"

Gently the quiet quilted clouds amass,
Crawling northward from a southern inlet rash,
Clinging gray to the indigo seam where the land meets the sea,
And lifting the wind in its haphazard front,
That grapples for my attention,
And here catches up with me.

*"Daddy, good, good. You have shifted. It happens, and now you
have shifted back ever so slightly. Your resilience amazes me. It
has got to be so hard for you to manage this back and forth. I see
it. I feel it. I hate this for you, but I see the bigger picture. I can
see where you are going and your destination. It is spectacular,
Daddy. I will never let you do this phase of your life without me.
Just keep walking with me. There's nobody else out here on this
stretch of beach. Just us. Take my hand, Daddy, I will guide you
through the trauma."*

"No Man's Land"

Shedding the skin and breathe the spine,
Dream web awake cannot haunt me,
Distraught and forlorn,
In the bloodied remnants of tattered human uniform;

I call for solace in sacrifice,
I beg of surrender,
Of surrendering arms,
The lamb caught on a ferocious field of fire,
Frantic panic fingers my only manic shovel,
Digging and ducking behind broken branches,
Yet I will not pass unharmed,
Running out of lucky second chances,
As the heated tongues of bullets hiss passed my eyes.

"Do It All Again"

Dream released appeased and narrow,
Seedlings of a broken arrow,
Teething on this seething marrow,
Would you, would you…

…Concede defeat of a dreary morrow,
Drenched in sheets of blackened sorrow,
And black sheets of funeral rain,
Aware that as today will be tomorrow,
Will you, will you…

…Recede replete and beaten at day's end,
Bruised and buckling beyond a mere mend,
Knowing that around the each night's bend,
You will have to do it all again,
Do it all again,
Do it all again,
Every day…

…Again.

"Monsoons Unhinged Within"

The rains shall come and blanket the earth,
And make rivers of mud from rich arid dirt,
Pooling into valley lakes of laughter,
That settle down but only…

…After the turmoil has taken its toll,
After the turmoil prompts erosions growth,
After the turmoil has reshaped this road,
After the turmoil has scaped this soul,
In the tormenting shape of grieving, bleeding river,
That floods within these corridors,
Like a great lake overflows a petite porcelain bowl.

"An Active Drowning"

There was an active drowning,
The last of my breath escaped my lungs,
With hundreds of feet still upward to travel,
The surface of the water as far away as the sun,
Swimming in this misery gulping for my life,
From morning until night mourning until night,
And then the sleep it slays me,
Succumbed to the slumbering cycle fight,
Until my eyes awaken to another morning…

…Without light;

For this is a nightmare from which you never awake,
A nightmare from which you never escape,
Tossing and turning in catastrophic fits to emerge,
But them comes another powerful surge,
Another layer of water that lays itself upon you,
Rising upward through this accumulating ocean of grief,
It grows by its nature in all that it subdues;

And nothing here can save me,
Nothing but a constant yearning to swim,
With hundreds of feet still upward to travel,
I want to, but I will not give in,
For this active drowning,
Is just the path forward…

…Toward the eternity within.

"Intending Into The Darkness"

    i.   *Black Sheets Of Night*

These black sheets of night they are raining,
Yet nether a teardrop slices the air,
Veils of sorrow overtake me,
Thunderstorms that eclipse towering despair,
I walk and I walk in this darkness,
Tempting the shadows across this windy mere,
For I know that in order for conquest,
These are the black sheets of night I must dare,
Intending into the unknown,
I intend this space to share;

    ii.   *A Dark Sandy Road*

Out over the dunes in the darkness,
Following shadows that quietly grow,
Into a darkness that clings to a blackness,
Blinded with vision, I see with the soul;

The sands underfoot shift in wind and reform,
Ever so slightly to change what I've known,
The desolate south end of Jekyll Island,
The longer I walk the deeper I go;

And here in this hallowed ground screaming,
The end of the world seems to unfold,
No one here to observe me or hear me,
Yet I am not alone;

The bobcats observe from the bushes,
The loggerheads lay their eggs in sandy knolls,
A sanctuary for nesting winged creatures,
The deer scatter through the palmettos;

Yet there is another quite present,
A sacred spirit, a holy soul,
My daughter walks me through the darkness,
Lining with light this dark sandy road;

 iii. *Inter-Dimensional*

In this constant barrage of misery,
Blanketed by grief's artillery,
I lie face down in a field of fire,
Zeroed into each inch of this mire,
The shrapnel clips the cloth that clothes my skin,
As the penetrating metal finds the easy was in,
A cushion for the perpetual pin,
My humanness is paper thin…

…Allegorically speaking I submit,
To that which I cannot resist,
A daily feast of physical losses,
And daily pinned to each new day's crosses,
I courageously find my way,
In this constant barrage of miserable pain,
To reach across this No Man's Land wire,
And find myself inter-dimensional,
As you take me higher and higher.

"Standing Staring At A Midnight Jungle Lush"

i.   Bracing For What's To Come

The storm belies a calmness in its developing front,
It draws down the temperature,
Chilling wetted skins,
It saturates with a quietude,
The tree line just before the hunt,
When all lies still in the forest,
And no prey dares its run,
I am standing in the calm before the storm,
And bracing for what's to come;

ii.   Grief Swamp

The swamp of grief is not easy terrain to traverse,
For the feet slung forward feel like stepping in reverse,
It is a sluggish bog of horrific sorrow,
It is itself in these woods a curse,
But what shall I do in this moment…

…I have only the next step through morass to struggle, trudge,
It is no better,
It is no worse;

iii.   Wilderness Impassable

This impassable wilderness from my mind to my mouth,
Though there be sketches of words,
I cannot seem to get them out,
In the tangle of the underbrush,
And although I scar the throat as I shout,
There is an impassable wilderness,
From my mind to my mouth.

"A Warrior Of Light"

Peering into the jaded mouth of the jagged teeth of sorrow,
And its swollen tidal waves of pain,
I calculate my limited options of denial or flight,
And instead dig in the heels;

And breathe slowly;

With a crashing rattle against the rocks,
I throw away my shield,
And grip my sword with both hands,
Lunging into the fray,
Gashing at the grief,
Slashing violently at the thief,
Cutting down this massive hurricane,
Into manageable waves.

"Daddy, I love this piece. I love how you fight. I love how you taught me how to fight. I learned how to fight back and take care of myself from you. Now relearn how to fight from me. We have inverted, as you said to me just after my transition. I have been leading you like our relationship of parent child has inverted to child parent. It cracks me up, actually, leading the man who is my beloved warrior father. How humbling. How wonderful. I love you, Daddy. Thank you for your courage."

"The Wave Is Coming"

i.   *Instinct And Shoulder*

The wave is coming,
I can see it with the eyes in the back of my head,
The wave is coming,
Larger than life and larger than death,
The wave is coming,
Its suffering like tsunami spills, spreads,
The wave is coming,
As the beachfront braces for its wrath,
The wave is coming,
Mooring my feet in the sand just before the collapse;

ii.   *Grief Breath*

Like a grenade exploding,
In the fleshy pond of the stomach bowl,
It's shrapnel blazing new gaps,
Through the internal terrain,
Blowing up algae,
Shale, slack and muck,
That decimates these holy corridors,
Breaking the rib cage and puncturing the lungs,
In its massive convulsion,
In the tortured repercussive nature of grief,
Like a tornado scores its mark in a vacuum,
An F4 rips through my chest,
Yet, as now, this is simply just a breath,
Forced in these days not like any other breath,
That in grief I am forced to breathe;

The wave is receding,
And pulling sands into the deep,
And pulling my feelings,
Draining white the blood from my feet,
For the wave is receding,
With the sentiments of man,
The wave slows, but is still retreating,
Revealing revelations,
Soiled with the chaotic sediments of man…

…All in six seconds of exhalation.

"Another 24 Hours"

I wake up to the crashing thunder,
I wake up to the straining spine,
I wake up just as it pulls me under,
I wake up where the sand finds its line;

I crawl into the roaring sunrise,
I crawl away from disheveled bed,
I crawl the path as the crow flies,
With a sacred vow to defend;

I walk the hours that cursed me blindness,
I walk the hours with clear intent,
I walk through grief and lashing sorrow,
I walk through black sheets of torment…

…And I always find you standing here;

I bed down in the fading midnight,
I bed down knowing that in another day,
We have together traveled in the fight,
To grow together in a loving grace…

…For despite your physical absence,
An accident you did not cause,
You arise in a spiritual presence,
Our relationship knows no pause…

…For I always find you standing here.

"The Sheep's Soft Clothes"

We trace the frames of treason,
On lips that tarnish paused,
Eclipsed amidst amassing sorrow,
To purge illicit cause,
Yet maybe we dream the dream,
We arrive like flotsam in the flux,
And maybe we dream so deeply,
It buckles the resolve we trust;

We brace against the cyclone,
With fibers twined into these walls,
And lastly crawl into the basement,
To shelter should this structure fall,
And buried then in this debris field,
We wear collapsed structure like a protective shawl,
And maybe dream will find us weeping,
Will anybody hear our calls;

We face the winds well warped and seasoned,
To find ourselves where lest we go,
And triage wounds that gape this spirit,
The tumbling shards of glass and stones,
That rip deep holes and gashes open,
That shred the skin to be disowned,
And maybe dream was nightmare hiding,
Underneath the sheep's soft clothes.

"Sounds No Human Should Make II"

Hugging the sand path rolling under tangling canopies,
In a perfect darkness, following the sound of the sea,
Flanked by shadows that obscure thick frames,
Of salt washed sprawling oak trees,
Tucking their arms into black leather sleeves;

Where the humidity moistens the trail,
With heated smoky steam,
Is where we will be discovered,
On a spiritual journey,
How hard the soul cries,
How sad the soul cries,
How loud the soul cries,
Making sounds no human should make…

…Louder each day away,
From the moment of physical brake.

"Escape Into Music"

Emotional adrenaline flurry the channels in tonal images,
Evocatively motivated to spur emotive ears,
It finds the strings that frame the heart,
And manipulates the thumping light,
As the music soothes the sacred soul,
In colorful contrast to a world willing to rip you apart,
The song it is itself life,
Like an additional heartbeat one may hold,
The song itself is rich with life,
And draws you deeply into its fold,
The song at last it with its sight,
Carries you safely…

…Down a dark and lonely road.

"The Shadow's Shade"

For the shade in the shadow,
It is as dark as it is deep,
When a mask wears a mask,
As slumber is to sleep,
I stagger up the box canyon,
With walls slick and steep,
And keep sliding back to the bottom,
In a bubbling, gurgling wounded heap;

For not the solid ground's stability,
Beyond the lip, endless possibilities,
And I yearn into its jagged mouth,
Lean into it willingly,
And fight to find another way out,
As the tension is slowly killing me,
And I swallow the sun,
Barbed lights full of unsheathed blades,
And the days they turn into…

…Itself the shadow's shade.

"Daddy, you can do this. You are walking, releasing, feeling, expressing, processing, shedding and screaming forward. You always told me, 'the only way through is through,' and you are walking through this darkness both inside the grief and out on this midnight summer beach. You are amazing to watch. Your clarity will come. You will feel me, hear me and see me better shortly. Remember what Nate said so wisely, 'Daddy, when you are between channels it proves that there are channels.' Keep walking, Daddy. Keep walking."

"Circles In Your Rooms"

Grief is the coal that fires my anger,
In an engine running cobalt blue,
Hotter than a red dwarf molting,
Shedding colors in atmospheric hues;

Holy the cradle where my arms cross,
Securely bundled I find you,
Little new baby girl gaze upon me,
Smiling swaddled in your safety suit;

I walked in circles in your nursery,
For hours staring at your sleeping face,
*"Father I am in dedication hallowed,
Bettered by the hours we together pace;"*

Fifteen years later this life in a flash,
Like lightning rash in cobalt blue,
I pace your teenage room in tears,
Walking in circles in hopes…

…To find you…

…And here upon this beach,
In spirit, now twenty one,
I am walking languishing long miles,
Like walking in circles on the sun,
Finding me standing…

…Where I had once begun.

"Saints, Martyrs and Angels"

We have in the maelstrom a burgeoning need,
It comes with emergent suffering and speed,
And in the stunning powerlessness,
When danger haunts a dank plateau,
When the dirge in the daylight streams hollow sound,
When the flaking emotion sheds a layer of skin,
Eroding the soul as river erodes porous grounds,
And in its flow the specter of grief grows,
And then the grief itself, release the hounds,
That range hunting through the soul,
Plodding with growling teeth,
Like a herd of stampeding razored buffalo,
Raising smoke trails over fertile fields,
And burning down the harvest promised yield,
To entertain the specter of starvation in the months to come,
As layers of soul away are peeled,
This,
This,
This is how I feel;

With pluck and purpose in a durable eye,
And sand underfoot where the dunes are dry,
I journey flanked with saints,
And this band of chosen angels,
Who flutter in and out of view,
Depending on the moon's angles,
Like diamond flashes in firelight,
And refracting rainbows sparkle just right,
I take these steps though the feet are strangled,
Like fallen oak branches twisted and mangled,
And run with the wild buffalo,
That range hunting through my soul.

"In A Season Of Subtle Signs"

Fatigue it come,
Clawing its way,
In through the circulation and catacombs of veins,
Searching out to strangle the mystic light;

Fatigue it inspects,
Circling for a weak spot to force a disconnect,
In through the shallow breath,
In through the pain,
In through the hallowed depths,
Of this human terrain;

In the season where signs,
Have been hidden sublime,
There is unrest, despair,
There is anger,
There are fountains of fear,
And signals of danger,
Beware, beware,
For the ground here…

…Is unstable;

It is not that she is not speaking,
It is not that she is not here,
It is something amiss,
In the way I misinterpret this atmosphere,
For the signs are all present,
It is I who cannot hear,
I will rest in the respite,
My child…

…And recollect my strength,
And take a new angle on this season,
Another jag in crackling jade of the grief road,
For although the signs are subtle right now…

…They are present nonetheless…

…And cleanse the mycelium,
And wash the spirit skin,
And bathe in the electric waters,
In the zone of saturation,
That sparks for attention,
In the chambers caged by chest,
And into the deep ever faithful,
We alight in our love ever blessed.

"An Interlude Of Empowerment"

Let us knock the bolts off of the doors,
Let us shake the rain from the cloud banks,
Let us scream in pain,
And dream in thanks,
Blistering, hold no vessel oasis,
Less than we have known,
Let us breach the lines fabricated,
That man has created,
Between the flesh and soul…

…Here in the interlude,
Insolvent of servitude,
Let us finally know…

…Here are the ways in which we travel,
Life alight in this worthy ship of life,
On the open oceans of eternity.

"Fifteen Purple Ribbons"

And just beyond the Glory walkway,
And we cross a familiar landmark,
In an obliterating darkness,
The path to chart through blinking stars,
Hearing the gentle call in the warm steady wind,
Rustling threads,
I lean closer and attempt to see with my hands,
Branch to branch;

Fifteen purple ribbons,
An accident at fifteen years old,
Fifteen purple ribbons,
A wind shaped tree holds these strips tied into bows,
A scraggly beach tree exhales and breathes,
For the father who tied these tiny strings,
For the father who here grieves,
For the daughter for whom his heart breaks,
Metal tears drip from rustling shells of leaves,
Fifteen ribbons tied into bows,
Snap and flutter in the breeze,
Purple ribbons tied into bows,
On the high dunes in a tree,
Purple ribbons tied into bows,
On last year's journey to the sea.

"Remember To Believe"

Passively I pardon me and pass You,
These are possibly the reasons,
For my faulty reprieve:

I am busied in this busy altitude,
For life and many seasons,
Has its complexities;

I am man,
A mountain in the middle of the ocean,
With slices of cliff faces melting,
Crumbling into the sea;

But I can't seem to see,
Beyond the fabric of me,
And what it is that constructs me;

And passively, aggressively, I pardon me,
And my selfish habits…

… But will You surface in my sight,
And rescue me…

…From me…

…Once I have had enough,
I remember to believe,
Oh God, I have had enough,
Come,
Come rescue me.

"Eternal Wounded"

I know we're not cursed, Dear,
But the perversity of logic is clear here,
Never more could a tragedy roost,
Than in the innocence of this rarified air,
Where a family struggles with making sense,
Where life has cast them false pretense,
Never more could my heart be wounded,
Than in the emptiness I now hold in my hands;

The deceiver is life itself,
Its deceit and its damage here deeply felt,
We were effortless in the morning,
And destroyed before midnight's bell,
And the breadth of destruction,
And the miles to trudge before I die,
Never more could my soul be wounded,
Than watching your life slip away from mine;

And now, God, we are standing here,
Facing each other in symbolic stare,
An accidental physical death,
In Your world where this is most unfair,
I rage at You and I also worship You,
For she is somehow standing right here,
And the miracle of her presence flowing,
The journey with my beautiful daughter is growing,
Thank you, Lord, for that mission of pity,
Though my soul, my soul, my soul…

…My soul, my soul, my soul…

…Is itself eternally wounded.

"Turning Back To The Path"

i.   In Anticipation Of Daily Growth

Lifted from the lethargy cables succumbed,
Like puppet strings strapped to uneven fulcrum,
I pitch and pivot and purge and molt,
And shed my skins like shedding coats,
Making space for remap and maneuver,
In anticipation of daily growth;

ii.   Softened By Belief

What are bags of jagged glass,
You have softened by Your sea,
What are seeds of our tomorrows,
You have spread in the settling breeze,
What are traumas tucked in torturous glaze,
That fake their stance as opportunities,
What are these bags of glass I am breathing,
Softened by belief;

iii.   Spirit Ears

With spirit ears into the rage I go,
With spirit ears into the fray,
With spirit ears the noise it simmers,
And boils off the edges of waves,
For spirit ears are keen antennas,
To lift one's hearing above the pain,
With spirit ears into the faith I go,
To hear calmly in the fray.

"Recital of Holy Verse"

Gifted by our Gentle King in the artistry of words,
In gratitude oration,
Our gift in return to our Holy King,
Is poetic verse,
Painting scenes of salvation,
And spiritual elation,
Into these emotive oceans we are immersed,
To wash away in the salty tidal waters,
All of our fears in which are linked the chains of this curse,
That lurk in our stomach lining,
That pock our wagging tongues with thirst,
In the fabric of human imperfection,
And the chambers of dejection,
The suffering is even worse…

…If only the ointment and bandage comes,
With the recital of holy words,
In the calming touch of poetic verse…

…I yearn its outcome as I proclaim,
The sounds no human should make,
The sounds no human should make,
The sounds no human should make,
Screaming out in Your name.

"The Hand In God's Hand Is My Daughter's Hand"

With the sound of my breath ripping out through the chest,
With the noise of anxiety deafening the ground,
Where the sacred soul is kept,
I flail and I fumble and fail and tumble,
And fade and stumble and twist tighter in this chaotic web…

…And all alone the tension roars,
Insufferably the engine pistons scorch,
Burning up the oil of humanity,
And igniting my flesh into a fiery torch;

It is always that I reach out for you,
In every single moment,
Not only when I can't take it anymore,
It is always your hand that guides me,
Just a few further frightful steps more,
It is always your hand in God's hand,
That is holding my hand with our Lord's.

THE WILD WHERE THE BOBCATS PRAY

The Sea And The Sand"

Into the wild where the bobcats play, there are spread two dozen Loggerhead nest posts; markers of sacred fluidity, God's markers on this tiny, tiny earth. There are tangles of mangled branches and weathered tree stumps, smoothed by the daily tides, reconfigured, splintered like delicate ocean bone or made to harden in the baking heat of the sun.

And so, Kayleigh, we tuck our heads under the bush and venture out onto our beach beyond the water tower. She has already passed, her prints baring northward. Soon she will turn south again, perhaps weaving in and amongst our footprints thoughtfully, in and out of the vegetation and the wild and the shadows lurking amongst the trees with their curving, winding, sea breeze shaped branches. Her home is magnificent, fit for a queen, and she, the bobcat queen, is humbled in her abode. Thought I cannot see her, she is here. Though I cannot see her, she sees us. Though I cannot see her, she is claiming dominion across the dimensions of dune and beach, of forest and open plain, of the sea and the sand.

"The Bobcat"

Trusting old soul bronzed with antiquity scrolls,
Ancient soul,
Wisdom collected traversed over forests,
And lives,
An angel guide's focus sharpens in bobcat's vision,
Fundamental fortitude,
Cunning,
Planning a means to a goal quietly,
Patient and calm, tenacious and strong,
Elusive and nocturnally kept,
Invisible to ignorance,
The secret keeper,
The Anam Chara,
Adaptable in co-existence,
Transformation and rebirth,
She can reinvigorate breath upon its death,
The domesticated cat of the Lord;

You are measured in your calculations,
Show me how to see in this darkness,
Unravel the truth from the brambles of man,
Tied to the backbone of the night,
Where security roams and instinct reigns,
You see what others cannot,
New life cycles abound in a chain of light,
In your eyes,
Your eyes…

"A Script Of Light"

Glittering flakes, salt to the taste,
The moon where the water refracts,
Has left shards of its face,
And the swirling ignites,
A million stars in the night,
The shimmering it makes…

…A water parchment where the angels write…

…On this scroll of love…

…A script of light.

"Tonight Eternal"

i)   Steam

Returned we have to the steam of contemplation,
Heated into gas,
Here beside the water's edge,
In a vapor trail of elevation,
We gasp, we cry, we whisper,
Though nobody else here stands,
Digging our toes in the sand…

ii)   Tonight Eternal

Tonight the air is as the sea is,
Wet with humidity,
Drenching the atmosphere,
Opening warmed pores;

The stars swim through this mist,
Their skins radiate with heat,
Tonight the air resists,
A watery release;

The silence echoes silence,
On the empty grounds the sounds of pounding waves,
They crash upon the barrier,
Where the pressure has escaped,
They collapse upon the barrier,
Loosen soul stones in the barricades,
As the silence finds an inroad,
The weakness in the daisy chain,
It screams until the eardrums bleed,
And chafes the spirit with immortal pain;

Tonight,
The sea is as the air is,
Warm with fluidity,
The moon casts dispersion,
Or acceptance,
Or convergence,
We know not,
Subjects of its fiery gaze,
It is blurred in the haze,
Upon the quiet glassy face,
Of an ocean that lay in a blackness,
Without the rhythm of its waves.

"Daddy, it is okay. Let's take a minute. Your legs are tired. Your muscles ache. Remember, the resting spots are your friend for in them you find your footing to elevate in your next steps. Its just as natural a process as your grief. Rest with me and let's gaze out to the ocean with no distraction of taking the next step. Let the next step be sitting and meditating and elevating with me. I love you so much, Daddy. Thank you so much for walking with me, being with me, sitting with me."

"Sitting With Kayleigh At Midnight On Our Dunes"

When the warmth threads itself with stillness,
In a seascape tapestry,
And the cloudless night sky reveals,
The bluish bands of the Milkey Way Galaxy,
A spirit rides across the crashing waves,
Pulsing at the edges of our faith,
She sits beside me staring up,
With youthful, hopeful, beautiful gaze;

That was the last time before the trauma,
We sat there together on the dunes,
When the accident a week later tolled,
It stole your physical presence,
And scathed the walls of my soul,
When you, my little girl, were physically killed,
Against your will,
Trying to just come home,
No day would thereafter ever be full;

Yet sitting with you at midnight,
Two chairs dig into white sand dunes,
And we breathe the ocean of stars,
And through its waves the swimming moon,
It glistens in our unwavering eyes,
On this road that we together choose,
Thought some might see but one human body…

…The other chair holds you.

*"Daddy, how quickly our meditation time together tolls. Fifteen
minutes. An hour. Sitting here together. I know my Daddy. You
want to get up and keeping going. Off into the darkness, Daddy.
Come on. Let's go explored!"*

"Walking On The Sun"

We together walk in a delicate silence,
The lapping of the waters has begun…

…On the backbone of St. Andrew's Sound,
Where the black waters run,
Where the tangle of branches and crabs and brackish sand,
Find my footsteps pressed in the ocean mud,
Crossing the sanctuary of the southern curve,
With Glory Beach in my lungs,
The bobcat calls in the distant trees,
The scrub brush hold its tongue,
As she teaches her cub the sacred cycle,
Of the sleep, the walk, the hunt…

…Walking together in silence,
In parallel to us,
Walking together in silence…

…Is like walking on the sun.

"When The Lion King Roars Run Toward His Mouth*"

I stare down the lion's throat each morning,
As it lurks and shrieks and strikes without warning;
I stare down the lion's throat every day,
With shield in hand and holding my blade;
I stare down the lion's throat each evening,
No matter how tired or the anguish in grieving;
I stare down the lion's throat each night,
For the only path forward is right through its fight;
I stare down the lion's throat in the dawn,
Like a warrior seizing the battlefield's calm;
And though sometimes I just want to throw up my soul…

…I search out the lion and tackle his throat.

When a lion king roars, its prey scampers away from its dangerous roar and unbeknownst directly into the path of the female lions who are waiting to do the killing. Analogously when grief strikes in a wave we want to run from it, but we are to turn on our heels, dig in, and run directly at the lion king, directly at the grief and take it head on.

"The Flesh Of Sword"

The sword is heavy fleshed in gilded steal,
Reinforced and bridled with heavy grief,
That strikes with the weight of how I feel,
And the blows are heavier,
Than few are the humans who can reveal;

Its enigmatic blade it drags on the rock,
And cuts a chasm a century deep,
Across each inch and each second,
With cliff faces that are ocean's deep,
Into which the thunder scurries,
Chasing this bottomless grief;

The flesh of sword is complicated,
Interlinked with cells of disbelief,
Jeweled with faith stones carved and jaded,
Torched and scarred with the puncture of Lion's teeth,
Earned in the battle of confrontation,
I aim to carry its head on a stick,
Tackling the ever-present and elusive beast,
To kill or be killed by this grief,
That leaves a soul both strangely strong and sick.

"In A Cloud Of Misty Air"

(i)   *The Shoreline*

Standing at the promised sheen of shoreline,
Curling ocean rise and flow toward me,
Whimsical rainbows webbed into the spray of the sea,
Waves that burst into the sand plain,
And disperse into a thousand water seeds,
That root into the wind,
And in the breeze disappear,
That grow into the folds,
Of a cloud of misty air;

(ii)   *Human Sea Shells*

The ocean waves become my bloodstream,
Organic and wild the flesh and floral streams,
Flow through the veins and channels and the capillaries,
That mesh and web together as me…

…But is it truly me;

The ocean waves become the air that I breathe,
Higher in vibration and devotion achieved,
Flow through these lungs that spirit unsheathes,
For human shell is a sea shell,
And little resembles me…

…What if I told you…

…But what if I told you it was me.

"A Ship Called Resilience"

We sail the rising face of typhoon,
Climbing into the slick rain skins of the sky,
And as the elastic sheets stretch to the threshold,
The crest of water mountain arrives;

And in the slacking plummet screaming,
And as the skiff blades itself down descending spine,
The hungry valley below, its mouth it opens,
To swallow the vessel in its ravenous eye;

And in the collision of wave and timber,
And as the grief and glory collide,
The fight continues across the torment,
A punishing sea carves the landscape wide,
Yet dream a sailor shapes with faith…

…Climbing, climbing, climbing…

…Into the rain skins of the sky;

Brittle teeth, bare fragile hold on this tether,
Where the fingernails stress at the point of fracture,
Yet hold the line where the soul's muscle shakes,
And strains at capacity;

An adjustment in the grasp,
Where the slippage was detected,
Before it increased you find a final grind,
Long enough to withstand the burn,
And soft enough to embrace it.

"Perpetual Spark"

And there it is in which we loiter…

…In the pale darkness at the speed of sight,
Staring into the sun to achieve the view of the shadows,
Of midnight,
Like cloaks of heavy cotton a mile wide,
And porous filigree bundles three miles thick,
Suffocating the horizon that squeaks for attention,
A fading golden lantern yearns through the cloud banks,
A signpost toward salvation,
A future under siege,
A familiar pattern,
Breathe,
Breathe,
Breathe;

Unearth, unbind these grievous eyes,
And embrace this unhindered hour…

…That lurks in the brightest powers…

…Within the flexing vacillation of your soul.

"The Moon Consumes The Blackness That Surrounds It"

Into the mouth of flowers breathe,
On the salty rib cage of tidal waves,
In the foaming webbing of salty filigree,
I submit to the rumbling dissonance,
That collapses the bars of this cage,
Mesmerize the typhoon in panicked eyes,
Just long enough to recognize,
That the heart with many moons may rise,
Yet still may feel empty…

…In the blackness it consumes.

"Daddy, how can it be any other way? The duality is itself constant tension; two things at once, those things being the penultimate happiness of a father's love for his child, and the total destruction and despair of that child's sudden physical death and absence. It breathes you. You breathe it. It mixes. Oil and water. It bleeds. It is hope and heartache. It is grief and glory. It is a constant opportunity to rise through the challenge and vibrate higher and higher. Dynamis vox vibrantem, Daddy, dynamis vox vibrantem! Love you!"

"The Emerald Moon (Claddagh Angel)"

She wears a smoky ring of wind around her finger,
A lace of light around her neck,
Gifted to her by her father,
Filled with the gold of sunrises and sunsets,
And deeper together they see farther,
Than one alone can detect,
They sit upon the beach at night,
And marvel at the green lunar flame,
That slowly crawls from east to west…

…Asking others…

Have you ever beheld the Emerald Moon,
Hands and heart and crown in bloom,
It bleeds when tears lay soul in ruins,
It screams to blaze a trail pursuing,
The pain as daylight is consumed,
By nighttime with its blackened hues,
And glowing across the seaside dunes,
To soothe our worst and deepest wounds,
Shines the promise…

…Of the Emerald Moon.

"In The Wild Ranges Of The Soul"

No matter the road,
We walk together,
No matter the challenge,
We walk its weather,
No matter the pain,
No matter the grief,
No matter the strain,
No wane in belief,
We walk together,
No matter the road,
We walk the weather,
That ranges the soul.

"Ultrasense Instinct"

Help me breathe with my eyes,
Help me see with my ears,
Help me hear with my senses,
And reach through my fears,
Help me be relentless,
Through the black sheets of tears;

Bewitched between a storm bank rising,
And a calmness crackling, fading,
Becalmed beneath a veil of sorrow,
And emotions degrading,
I find myself in this cyclical pattern,
Through swamps of torture wading,
And sinking nonetheless,
With each step I am taking,
But what other option exists,
Though my heart is breaking,
I trudge upon this road,
And persist,
Persist,
Persist;

Rejoice in the rebalance,
Rebalance in the reroute,
Reroute in the challenge,
This challenge to live and rejoice,
And balance somehow,
For there is no other choice,
And choose an audience of light,
Emerging from the darkest corners of my fear.

"Diamond Knives"

Teardrops cascade,
Swell into tidal waves,
That collapse onto beach into steam;

And moonbeam it cries,
With its diamond knives,
That twist shells into opal sleeves…

…While I quietly grieve…

…Gasping, the dying in each breath tolls,
Grasping for footing where the sand dunes roll,
And dry apart,
This is the last frontier,
Of a broken heart,
This is the last frontier,
Of a broken heart;

…And diamond knives,
They carve into the blackness,
And dull themselves the blades of shining stars,
Of all that we have been,
And all that we are,
For this is the last frontier,
Of the broken heart,
For this is the massive fear,
In the reigns of the broken heart.

"Harmony"

(i)   Accelerate

I want to accelerate with you,
Integrate ideas and blend with your vision,
I want to rise with your rising,
Despite my soul's shrapnel incision,
I want to breathe the air you are breathing,
Even though my heart is heavy in grieving,
I want to accelerate along the path,
Where faith births from the toil of believing,
And believing is our home;

(ii)   For Harmony

I sympathize with harmony attuned,
I realize alarmingly that I am subdued,
I symbolize the harrowing deep bruise,
And recognize the depths that it pursues;

And into the soul lining it captures my light,
And without the soul I would give up the fight,
And without the soul I would surrender my life,
And so I must triage the soul to renew,
And bandage the wounds and the scars and deep bruise,
And root out the depths it pursues,
And realize that if I remain subdued,
Then I would not champion this pursuit…

…For harmony…

…For you.

"Channeling The Wind"

Bluish-brown webbed sea breathes tumbling sound,
As the wind blows a lace curtain shroud,
And opens a million doors,
And hidden windows along these shores,
Where the possibilities are endless,
For life itself is endless,
When the chances are explored…

…Life itself, befriend this,
Where the ceiling is just another cloudy floor,
And opens to another million doors,
That lead in every direction,
Awaiting courageous inspection,
For what in the wind may be found,
In the mist of the sacred sea,
In the mystery of tumbling sound,
It is the glowing figure of an angel,
My daughter,
Beautiful, miraculous…

…Profound.

"An Angel At Play"

Sage the aft light,
Burn the incense to the sky,
Aurora borealis,
Has erupted in the seams where the worlds collide;

Was it really the wind,
Or an angel at play,
That created this skyscape,
And brilliant display;

Mystic lights sparkle like fire confetti in the sky,
As blinding as a sun washed day,
Eruption of silky garments,
Wafting in a dazzling display;

An ode to an active period of seismic activity,
Caught in the blast of Geomagnetic storm,
A blistering disturbance in the Earth's magnetic field,
Bursting forth from solar winds,
And the delicate structure of the interplanetary fields,
When coronal emotion triggered on a heated angst,
Ejected from the sun,
A sun we cannot in the nighttime see,
Energetic explosion of light,
Solar material and energy becomes itself the sea,
That becomes a mystic playground,
For an angel to use…

…To reach her hand across to me.

"The Vigilant Pelican"

Forget not His perpetual flight;

The Pelican opens his wings and closes out the day,
He takes another stroke and the night is wiped away,
He banks across the Eastern sea and sunrise awakes,
He swoops Westward aloft and brings the dusk in his wake,
He moors the horizon in the crux of the midday,
And takes to the sky with vigilance while the sleepers lay,
Minutes to midnight where fear is testing faith,
Holding this beach under wing and in His claim,
For those of us,
Those of us...

...Who sing His praise;

I am here, Good Pelican,
With my daughter in her body of light,
Two souls walking the south end of Jekyll Island,
Walking the breathing glands of the living night,
We hear You and we feel You,
In Your perpetual flight,
We love You, Good Pelican,
And live in Your life.

"He loves you, Daddy, like no other can love, even more so than me and that is a lot! He knows your path, your pain, your passion. He knows the trauma that has befallen you. He see your resilient faith. In those moments, and there are many, when breath fails you, when you scream in screeches of sounds no human should make, know that He is present, ever present. And in that presence, Daddy, I am blessed with you too."

"A Pocket Of Clear Midnight Sky"

Distantly faint,
The darkest gray paint,
These black sheets of earnest rain,
Like oily veils smudge the sky deep at sea,
Where the lightning flees,
Escaping the pressure of misery;

And the midnight seaside clouds,
Like billowing velvet shrouds,
Turn back where the cooler winds touch the beach,
Beseeched…

…And there in the clear night above, the stars,
Blink undisturbed from the sea storms afar…

…Wrestling the coil from the hands of the night.

"Digesting Constructs"

Help me digest the confusing constructs of this day,
Help me process its geospatial mirages,
Corralled into acidic deposits,
That stick to my feet,
That are pocked, panicked and toxic,
That show me a path forward,
And then, like a monster, block it;

Help me digest the fabrications in my way,
And walk through the grief…

…Into the waking glade of your hands.

"Duality"

(i)   Intrigue and Balance

We celebrate and we suffer,
Not one without the other,
Should it be the case in this,
Then we would just be smothered,
For duality must exist,
In this case like none other,
We celebrate as we can,
And still, alas, we suffer;

(ii)   Still Alive

Crisscross the illusory divide,
Crisscross the apparent divide,
For there is no division,
None between our lives,
Only a changing of bodies,
Though still our souls survive,
Only a changing of bodies,
Though still our love here thrives,
Only a changing of bodies, My Love,
For you are still alive;

(iii)   Duality's Rebalance

We calibrate and recalibrate,
One into the other,
Two dimensional realities,
Intersecting halos and holy atmospheres,
Though recalcitrant the human plies,
Until the rebalance holds me,
In the calming cradle of your penetrating eyes.

"An Open Door"

(i)   Walking

Walk with me the stars alight,
When the deep space air opens up the massive night,
When the clouds disperse to distant shores,
Where there is much to be explored,
Together;

Walk with me the stars abloom,
Enchanted by the waning moon,
When silence erupts in quiet roar,
And orchestrates an open door,
Through which we walk together;

(ii)   Beyond The Limits Of A Limited World

And words, and worries, these lessons,
Shards that piece together jagged sea shell road,
Like jumbled messages on crumpled paper,
That make sense when they unfold,
Like a sparkling magic golden highway,
That lines the pathway to illuminate the soul,
You bring me guidance,
Sight in a world of blindness,
To help me see farther than my eyes can see,
Beyond the limits of this limited world.

"Sea Angels"

My bare feet melt in deep warm, white, soft sand,
For miles and miles overland,
My pores flush and breathe the boil of a lush southern night,
And its effervescent resonating sea…

…And the muscles they quiver and shake,
And the joints crack and ache,
Ten miles back and forth,
While I listen for the earth's release…

…Awaken to the angels on the breeze,
Slowing me kindly,
Before me, beside me, behind me,
Their majesty, it flourish,
Until I tire to my bones gripping collapse of the knees,
Finding,
As I sink into the exhaustion…

…An irresistible echoing chime of peace.

"A Mile North Of Glory Beach"

There is a little divot in the heavy pitched dune,
Spreading northward,
Where a tangle of trees by the high tide is consumed;

It bows inward and upward in the darkness,
Rooting palmettos and sea oats,
Where the morning glory bloom;

A little crease for a turtle nest,
A darkened corner where the bobcats rest,
Here along a heavy pitched dune;

That is where I sit to rest with my daughter,
My back against a sandy wall,
Branches over my head dance in crooked sprawl,
While I sip my bottle of water,
The night creatures in the shadows crawl,
And I rest to gather my strength…

…Before our midnight walk resumes.

"Illuminate Me"

A coastline frontier of lively brackish waters,
At night is as dark as the dark matter in space defies,
When then intermixed I see two oceans,
When I close my tired, hopeful, wounded eyes,
And trip across the axis,
When my defenses are crippled and torn,
From one dimension to another Atlantic,
And find myself sitting in Exuma Infinite,
Lustrous, endless, enchanted;

A coastline of crystal clear water,
At night is as dark as moonless sky,
Awaiting the flush of morning light,
For the turquoise colors to rise,
There is no difference itself in the waters,
Only that effect when light with it collides,
Illuminate me, my bright daughter,
For my waters are as dark…

…As moonless midnight tides.

"I Am This Quantum River"

(i)   A Golden River…

Foretell the toiling tremors,
Like a fault line in the soul,
And the soil vibrates and crumbles,
As the earth releases gold,
In the basin veins are emptied,
They banter sunlight in water folds,
Make sure that the river you offer up,
Has within it a liquid glow,
For the wind cries of late,
And the shade catches hold,
Were it not for this burning flame,
The embers would just grow cold…

…I know,
For the sorrow saps the sea line,
For the sorrow has its own road,
And the sorrow poisons this golden river,
Like a fault line in the soul,
But the sounds no human should make,
Erupt from a quantum crucible,
And a star on the edge of the universe cries,
With its impacted molecules;

(ii)   Spirit River

I am this spirit river that flows unto the sea,
Filled with human joy and human debris,
Filled with hope and promise and misery,
I am this spirit river…

…Wounded, flowing onward aggrieved;

Take my troubles, my tortures, my toxins,
Take from me my pain and poison and panic,
And these paper paradoxes,
Stepping into the wave break in willing accord,
Stepping into the entangled Atlantic,
Screaming at the water's edge…

…And sinking in the sand at its shore;

When I am speaking I hear little,
When I listen I seem to see,
When I hear you I am lifted,
Above the grief that chains my feet,
Feed me to the ocean,
Fill me with belief,
Pry apart my spirit river,
Cry apart my spirit river,
Open up my spirit river,
And bleed into the sea;

    (iii)   Quantum Entanglement

It is just by illustrative analogy,
A law as alive as the law of life itself,
"Daddy, I call to you in spiritual voice,
And instantly the words are felt,
I call you across the dimensions,
Where time and space are felled,
I radiate the highest vibration of love,
And your chest rises and your breath expels,
I love you and you love me,
And the entanglement is compelled,
To touch us both simultaneously,
in the laws of love itself."

"A Closing Of The Eyes"

We breathe deep dreams of coastal waters,
That stream through our open bodies,
Like a wave of divine light,
Scented with the fragrance of true perception,
That only comes once we close our eyes…

…And see the turquoise water that flows under our feet.

"Daddy, you know, all of these oceans are of one life. All of these dimensions are of one intersect. All of our lives are pressed into light and illuminate the kingdom of Life; life in the physical and life in the spiritual, with no break, with no severance, no solitude, no waiting. Are we not together right now walking and resting on this beach? Rejoice and be with your daughter in the Second Truth, though you grieve me in the First Truth. Parent me. Direct me. Guide me. Just as I daughter you, direct you, guide you and walk by your side; one in the physical and one in the spiritual, but together nonetheless. Come, keep walking. Love you!"

"Of The Mystic Sea"

Wispy, lush aster gardens tucked into the wind,
Blanket with scent of crushed lavender mint,
This coastal darkness christening accord,
With orange moonlight in fading golden tint;

Wrapping its halo piercing clouds and echoed shore,
While just beyond the tidal crashing din,
Of collapsing waves as each comes in,
An angel glides through diamond flashing doors;

Touching walker on the crown of his hair,
And hugging him while he embraces despair,
Forgetting he was not alone out here,
She finds the shallows in the dimensions…

…And in through breach she fords;

Weeping in the contact he smiles and he screams,
A bifurcated pain mixed with brilliant peace,
He misses her terribly physically,
Yet communes with her spiritually,
Daily,
In cathartic release;

He hugs the figure framed in the light,
In the doorway of the mystic sea,
Unveiled in a holy night,
Embracing the gap where the worlds they meet…

…And holds his daughter faithfully.

"For You Are Alive"

The moon, its hue now royal,
In a dark purple Catholic incantation,
Golden flowers of liquid fire light,
Its paschal reflection,
Petals of illumination,
The sky and the sea connection,
Moving as one organism;

Blooming galaxies sparkle like glimmering diamonds,
Stalked in long shafts of silver weaving warm rain,
And rooted into the firmament of eternal summer air,
Where the sea meets the sky,
Where the sea is the sky,
And the sky is the sea,
I feel the blanket of warm and sacred breeze,
Cover me,
And breathe…

…This breeze is yours,
And I believe…

…For even if my eyes cannot see,
My soul can always perceive,
For it is my pair of eyes,
And you, you sweet, Kayleigh,
You are alive.

"Eternal Hope"

If hope may spring eternal,
Then fear less the fearful pith of flagrant tides,
And wipe the mask of its grease paint complexion,
Of its worry scars and tearful lines,
And deeply reach into perfection,
And into faithful calm we rise,
With bitter pain and introspection,
The wisdom pulse has spurned the wise,
Through heartache brimming mountains,
And valleys as painful as the soul is wide,
Hope it then comes into view,
A watery spring flows like fountain,
From a crevasse in the cracks of the rock…

…Which are at last inspection,
Just the human cracks of man.

"The Dream Keepers Of The Beach"

The threadbare strings of smoky haze,
It hangs on the ocean on sunny days,
While we walk along the seashore,
Always, always wanting more,
And dream keeper work to weave,
The cords of faith and strings of belief,
It is all I can do to breathe,
To choke through this breath of grief…

…But as I turn to this empty space looming,
Where your physical body once occupied,
I see you standing in a grander light,
In the way the sun blinds my eyes;

There is more to this life than flesh and bone,
You tell me, you teach me that I am never alone,
Combing the beach for miracles,
That collect at our feet like sea shells tidal thrown,
Singing shells ringing together like tiny bells,
Reds and golds and flourished greens,
And purples and indigo shades of steam,
And orange and pink and pastel songs,
Drift along this oceanfront,
Like rainbow clouds we can barely see,
We sit and watch the parade…

…You and me,
The dream keepers that weave,
The physical and the spiritual lives,
Like twining together faith and belief,
And in your presence I loosely breathe,
To the best of each breath of grief.

"Vision Listener"

A torch flakes in the troubled tinderbox,
Awakening explosive flame,
I find the longest journey,
Finds my soul at odds with my own name,
Some days with sentiment buried,
Some days I trudge digging heals into the dream,
Some days I linger in the worry,
That webs and sticks like gummy sap to me,
Along, alone, the edge it barely,
Gives enough room for my own feet…

…Untie the breath and untether the eyes,
And in the reset realize…

…Visual touch and envisioned embrace,
Vision listener,
I hear your grace,
A voice of light it glows here,
A voice of light here resonates,
Amidst the elevation,
A loud, comforting vibration,
In the heartbeat of salvation,
I see your brilliant face;

I will carve out a brand new day,
In this crackling humid night,
Shoveled with my own bare hands,
I will construct from a misery maze,
A clarity platform on which to stand,
For more I am a spirit,
Than that I am a man.

"Hands Upon The Glassy Light"

Pressed against the glassy lights of Heaven,
Yearning through the static and the elastic of blue ether,
Dreaming of the higher life,
With my hands warmed by its steam;

Eclipsed not in symbolic mesh of lacy, porous veil,
More like the subtle landscape change,
From rolling dune to flattened beach,
Where the sands are all the same;

While the trumpets in the gardens play,
In the epochs of my human pain,
Plenty is the glory christened,
If I can manage the suffering day to day;

Pressed against the glassy lights of Heaven,
Yearning for her claim,
I hear the laughter of my daughter,
I yearn upon that final brilliant human day,
When I too submerge into the light…

…Of living water…

…And remain;

But for now the next door,
It leads to a higher elation,
Although I remain in my human flesh,
My soul resonates with this maximum vibration.

MAGNUS VIBRANTUM

"A Midnight Hummingbird"

She bounces tree to tree above us, Kayleigh. I cannot see her, but I feel her. I feel her so clearly. She is so close I can hear the rapidity of her wings funnel in my ear. I can feel the displacement of air beneath her feathered frame.

On a quiet wind, a messenger of joy, of love; intuitive the blessing. This mighty soul, yet a very tiny bird in stature; she is playfulness, gentleness, and beautiful resilience. Her message is clear: though the smallest of birds, she may be the strongest, beating her angel wings more than sixty times per second, dynamically flapping rainbow hued feathers of hope and the boisterous colors of life. There is no stagnation in her. There is only movement and observable joy in embracing the moment she beckons. She can stop immediately during fast, full flight. She can fly backwards and vertically, forward, up, down, and perhaps in circles and maybe upside down. She leaves tracers that I cannot see of infinity maps in the figure eight eternal patterns of her wings that paint on the wind. Happiness vibrates in her fast paced, brilliant energy. She is extra excited tonight for we are here with her. She knows that off in the distance, in that pitched black darkness of the south end of Jekyll Island's waters, a traveler will soon press her flippers to the sands, deposited on the beach in the surf, with the sacred cycle in her heart, crawling slowly toward the high dune line. Loggerhead. She is out there in the waters. Will we sync our steps in accord.

"Bobcats And Spirits"

On that stretch of beach where the bobcats play,
Where minutes apart our footsteps interlace,
Sharing a deep darkness in this wild space,
Pressing our feet into the beach's sandy face;

She watches perched in treetop,
With a keen and distance gaze,
Quiet and inconspicuous,
Content to disengage,
This is her jungle,
This is her forest,
This is her home,
This is her space;

And others gather on this isolated stretch,
Ancestors, my father, and others deeply blessed,
Gathered and led by the one I mostly know,
My daughter who rallies the family,
To comfort her father's broken soul;

On this stretch of beach where the spirit's play,
And the bobcats with my steps interlace,
Sharing a deep darkness in this special place,
Where even our angels press their feet into its face.

"Soul Cradle"

And shedding halos within halos,
These electric second skins,
Layer after vapor layer,
Peeling colors drawing in,
The deeper I go,
Toward the pulsing light within,
The more hallowed these steps,
Until the veil is so thin,
That I am standing in the cradle,
Where the spark of life begins.

"We"

i.   We Are Of Wind

I see the wind,
I hear its voice,
I breathe this wind,
This wind by choice,
I feel this wind,
In every void,
I breathe this wind,
That sings of joy;

ii.   We Are Of Ocean

I dream in blue,
I dream the sea,
And it is true,
It is of me,
These dreams of blue,
Are factually,
Just walks with you,
And walks with me;

iii.   We Of Sacred Beach

Our tangling bush and dunes for one week,
Our desolate trail through the jungle ford,
Our thankful hearts with the ocean speak,
Our souls tethered in unbroken accord,
A place without a postcard seek,
Along this rugged stretch of shore,
For here upon our sacred beach,
We find ourselves even more.

"Jekyll Island"

Where the spiritual world gathers to nest,
Where the spirit of the sea speaks to the soul,
Feel the turquoise electric salt waters traverse the air,
At the behest of God's ancient scrolls,
With sands of enigma in dune lines hum,
To the cycles of the moon and her tidal drum,
It is here where signs of Heaven like sea shells collect…

…It is here that we have come.

"Daddy, at different times in time we each have carried each other. For years. For centuries. We are alive in eternity, immortal beings in Gods country. And Gods country is big! Now in this moment of eternity, we are here on our sacred beach, walking and talking, elevating in time together, with so many blessings of communion. So many! Keep walking, Father. Let's turn back at the tower and search this stretch of beach again. The sea turtles love us. I'm sure our patience will find us with one of them soon. Love you!"

"The Stars"

We look to the stars, sea shells on another plain, which swarm in mighty galaxies in unwavering skies. We look to the stars, with their nebula trails, metallic sparkles, wisdom swirls of organic life, and miracle dust that finds itself into every ethereal crevasse in the universe. There are oceans, water canvas buoyantly holding the stars, and vast seas within the terrain of the stars themselves. Bleeding light and water.

Angels play in the carnival strings of glittering lights, loud in their intention, attentive to guiding vocals that reach an audience of open communion. We raise our eyes to these constellations, these galaxies, these planets, these tiny specks of dust and sigh into the mouth of its everchanging ocean.

Hummingbirds buzz in vibration crossing glowing globes, sphere to fiery sphere, feeding on the stars, and cross-pollinating adaptively environment to environment, dimension to dimension, heart to heart, soul to soul. They travel among what seem to be stagnant dots, these bonfires of the night that are in constant motion and breathing through the chains of evolution and spiritual machinery.

We look to the stars and find them exactly where our eyes have always looked. Within.

"Star Skin"

    (i)   Wind Path
Listening for the path through the trees,
The voices of fawning spirits,
In their amber freckled leaves,
Writing poetry inked in clouds,
Following the wind by its breeze,
Sensing the flow of the pull of the soul,
Where the dimensions into each other fold,
I see the framing of its door,
Cutting light beaming in the air,
Welcoming me,
And I enter the wind path,
By entering the grace of its peace;

    (ii)   Lunar Corona
In the deepening rash of a thunder heat,
The auras of auroras are shaken,
In the lavish tongue as the thunder speaks,
The enchanted midnight hour awakened,
Water droplets float in the atmosphere,
Invisibly,
Out over the charged oasis of the sea,
Liberally,
Where the weight of humidity is breaking,
Shedding ribbons of light in decadent dream,
Birthing radiant rainbows,
In the moonlight's diffusive diffraction,
Where comes the angelic sound of light,
In the gospel of the wind,
And in the scripture of the night;

(iii)   The Eyes Of Eternity

The hallowed stars in the water call,
Like an active parent,
Translucent, transparent,
Each galaxy a crystal of salt,
Fire sun seeds sprinkle and dance,
Ever charmed on an advancing wave,
While the moon's lustrous mystery,
Mixes, ministers and cascades,
Blending into the endless eyes of eternity,
That here view the ocean's break;

Star skin resides just under human skin,
Veined through dermis and subcutaneous lace,
Star skin plies and kneads human condition,
Its release our illustrious fate,
Each of us with sparkling ashes of stars,
Spread our light across the open space,
Unhindered, upheld by organic cage,
Once our human cells give way,
And our star skins take over,
And take their place.

"We Are God's Universe"

The stars are stepping stones across an ocean of dreams, across wide open seas that range through the soul from infinite endlessness to infinite endlessness. These stars are beacons, torches that light a path for us to traverse life to life, light to light. These stars are bright points of great mirages, great mystery, for they are not points of light at all, but galaxies themselves filled with millions of stars, millions of points of light each. That is the mystery, the miracle. The soul is much larger than it seems, much more infinite than the mighty dream of the universe. We are the stars. We are the light. We are the life that pulses through time and space. We are the universe. We are. And we rest like little sacred hummingbirds in God's loving palms.

"Unconquerable"

With eyes skinned with human limits,
We scaled the frail failing sunset,
Its withdrawing pastel raindrops,
Distracted our ways,
With its temporary scarlet haze,
But that was hours ago,
Days within hours ago,
Years within hours ago,
Centuries within hours ago;

And sparkle as they are swallowed by the gloom,
And masked we step into the boundary,
Of night lest the knife we forget,
The dream it left its rash on amber encrusted cloud banks,
Draped in roseate gold thunder stains of the blood of life,
While the perpetual fire radiates,
Revealing the immortal memory,
That pulses through the wounds…

…And speaks untarnished,
Of the conquering nature…

…Of our brilliant souls,
My child.

"Clouds Of Cerulean Gray"

Deep midnight gray,
The bands bend and the cumulous are spreading,
The blinking lights of the Sesnas play,
Against the star fields and the greater galaxy webbing;

In the humidity of a radiant summer's heatwave,
In the sweat of shouldered restraint,
I plod a course and forward strain,
Leave in my wake the marks of human stain,
Footprints dragging through the sand,
Dune after dune of dry and arid land;

Open my third ear to the sounds that exist beyond me,
In the ranging wounded rivers that pulse on my teeth,
Where the spirit horses run wild in the mist,
Pounding dust into clouds of cerulean gray,
Trapped in the funnel of the Brunswick bay,
As you tenderly take me by the wrist,
And point me toward a certain release,
A certain pursuit,
I will know once I have reached…

…Once I have reached…

…You.

"Fingerprints"

i.   Glow Upon The Crown

Washing your fingers through my hair,
Combing my beachfront crown gently,
Opening the window to the soul,
Where the dune skins,
And the living breathing waters flow,
And speak,
Where the intercession in its peaceful glow,
Moves my hair as you reach,
Across the dimensions to touch me,
Across these dimensions,
We breathe;

ii.   Alive And Present

See with my senses reeling,
What is it that I am feeling,
You…

…Truly you, as the air is my witness,
Though so many people do not get this,
You are here,
It is you…

…Touching my hair with your gentle fingers,
My daughter, as my life aches and lingers,
You intercede in miraculous ways,
You intersect the apparent divide,
For you truly are…

…Alive.

"The Scent Of Exuma Infinite"

The heavenly scent of Exuma Infinite is interlaced with the sugary smell of turquoise salt, powered on an ocean fresh breeze, and mixed with freshly blooming fragrant lilac. It overpowers the senses. It blends sight, smell, taste, touch, thought, hearing, feeling, knowing, believing, trusting and being. It is ever present, passing in with each inhale, floating as flows a river of light through the soul, and out into the brilliance of life with each exhale;

The soft linen woven breeze of Heaven like the exhaling breath of the ocean ebbs and flows across these brownish-blue Georgia waters; richly nutrient, funding magical summer thunderstorms, always intermixed with the spirit of the land;

These oceans are two as one, two at once; two dimensions, one from two; in the infinite finality the breath of life in the only breath we together breathe.

"Daddy, lift your vibration. Just a little bit higher. You will see me better. Hear me better. Feel me more presently. Be here with me in the elevation. Good. Good. Breathe in the light, Daddy, and feel its presence. The world is larger than the eyes can see. The world is larger than the heart can feel. The world is larger than the hands can feel. In the elevation your eyes scan deeper, seeing between the air, seeing through the air with feeling, feeling with your soul. Daddy, I am right here. Look out to sea! Do you see them both? Look at this beauty! These are our beaches! These are our oceans! This is us! Love you!"

"Two Beaches At Once"

I sit on two beaches simultaneously,
One setting leaves me vulnerable,
To the dangerous winds of physical life,
And one sitting finds me safely,
On a spirit seaside,
Secure in your arms,
Away from all harms,
Where the purple sky and the turquoise sea,
And the white sands and the glassy tides,
Greet me,
Where the angel osprey glide,
Where you sit by my side,
Smiling,
Your long blonde hair blowing in the wind,
Brushes gently across my shoulder,
Goosebumps ply the skin,
Where you help me find,
While sitting on two beaches simultaneously…

…How very much so the veil is thin,
How very much so the veil is thin,
How very much so the veil is thin…

"A Transition Of Scenes"

Streaming lightning sparkling, explosive green,
It radiates and disperses into steam,
Emerald diamond shards fire off into the glow,
That bursts through a turquoise sea,
It pounds like the pulsing of the heart,
That pushes the ocean through me,
Forced, flowing through my veins,
These golden veins,
Where the soul is its own cry of freedom,
Where the soul unhindered reigns,
Where the waters are living breath,
Where there is no death,
No death,
But a transition of scenes,
As the streaming lightning sparkles…

…God Himself, with purpose, speaks,
And charts a roadmap home…

…Through the power of His turquoise sea.

"Meditation"

i.   Water Meditation

I am water,
I am light,
I am breath,
The breath of life,
I breathe water,
I breathe light,
I breathe love,
Into this life;

ii.   In A Seaside Warmth

The smell of seaside turquoise warmth,
It is the scent of heavenly life,
The fragrance of a turquoise breeze,
It sends the senses ascending alight,
The perfume in a turquoise breath,
It blends together soul and sight,
For here together in this seaside warmth,
We celebrate new heights;

iii.   True Life

For I am itself water,
Though I am human despite,
I am empowered with the breath of God,
The breath of Higher Life,
For I breathe perfect water,
I believe in its light,
I weave together faith and hope,
That frames this temporary human life.

"Fuchsia Planets"

There are dream moons circling fuchsia planets,
And icy glitter rings that sparkle in sky blue galactic haze,
There are gardens that flow from fountains of light,
And open plains where wild horses graze,
In the valleys of the higher life,
Like turning in this book a simple page,
There are memories of that higher life,
I lose sight of as I age,
Yet cyclically the lives we've made,
Escape the grip of the lower cage,
And lift where there are dream moons circling,
Those fuchsia planets blessed by saints.

"SW3 (The Tracers Of The Night)"

Passing through the emerald shawls of a broken comet,
Turn my eyes to the sky,
Or to my side,
Or unaware remain I,
A quickly flash and sparkle,
A radiating dispersive flight,
A blast of white lightning,
Debris dissolves into light,
Crashing through the earth's atmosphere,
Or did we crash into its life,
Pushing our way through its dusty tail,
As if it was our right,
We walk within the emerald shawls of an obliterated comet,
Its icy fire hail,
That leads us down the spine of its back,
These tracers of the night,
That leads us down a sandy path,
Our bioluminescent footprints,
That trace the imprint of our lives.

"NGC 3631"

Could you travel 53 million light years in a breath,
As close to earth as life is weaved to death,
In the sway of Ursa Major emerges this celestial design,
With star arms that hug the entire galaxy organism,
With sparkling prisms of the holy divine;

Regions of illumination and nurseries ablaze,
And dark smoky nebula where the space fog reigns,
Intersperse across the paths of spirit guides,
Who leave messages in the logjam of matter,
In the gravitational collapse that comes with time;

Birthing new stars in a string of prayer beads,
Exuma psalms on parchment beach,
Shining green and bright bluish white,
A blending of visible and infrared light,
No human eye may detect,
While the soul sees…

…Endless life.

"The Winds of Exuma"

The scent of turquoise in the air,
And ocean waters calm and clear,
The breeze it carries with it prayer,
And bright white sands from auroral flare,
Exuma Infinite speaks in spirit tongues,
And spreads across the everywhere,
And when enlightened by its Heaven sun,
It is then I see her clearly standing here…

…Right beside me here,
Right beside me here,
Right beside me here.

"Okay, Daddy, now you are centered. Good work, Daddy, good job. Now elevate. Elevate. Take a breath and rise. You can do it, Daddy, you can do it. I know you and I know you can do it. You hear me. You feel me. You see me. Let go and elevate in a higher vibration. Love you!"

"Turquoise Lilacs"

Where a million nebula webbing elastically glows,
In a netting woven into star patterned clothes,
In the purple pinwheel galaxy spokes,
That spin on the engine so quickly the eyes choke,
This, the spirit road clawed out by this soul;

Turquoise lilac on a saltwater bloom,
Like the aqua blue fire sparked midnight summer moon,
The scent whistles in the reeds lifting,
To the sacred songs of nimble angels,
Weaving blessings in whispered strings of sound,
Like liquid diamonds seeped in sun glistening,
Carrying me to a higher ground,
Where the vibration of perfect light is shifting,
Illuminating turquoise lilacs…

…That float on a saltwater bloom,
In her eyes,
Somewhere on this spirit road,
Is somewhere by my side.

"Reverence"

Placing flowers of light at the feet of angels,
Wishing them soft prayers as small mementos,
Weaving an ever expansive tapestry of love,
Threaded person to person through the tolling centuries,
And the intersections of our interplanetary gardens,
And one thousand moons may treble and wax,
Where we grow brilliant flowers of glowing light,
And place them for each other,
At the feet of angels…

…To the smiling gentle pulse of our hearts.

"Elevated"

I am told the rise will wake me,
I am told these lives will never break me,
I am told these eyes though they are aching,
Will never fail the hour we are making,
Together,
Together,
My Love…

I am told in faith I enlighten,
I am told though waves may heighten,
And though I may be frightened,
This path will hold,
This path we line with gold,
Will hold,
My Love…

My little girl the world has harmed me,
Your innocent physical death destroyed me,
A debris field eviscerated,
Yet your spiritual presence charms me,
And gives me just enough room to breathe,
To see though my eyes seethe,
To scream, to mourn, to grieve,
To be where you are next to me,
Elevated,
My Love,
Elevated,
Across a cord of unbreakable light we together weave.

"Underneath The Water Tower"

I look out to this life and into its mouth a black hole,
In the void there is a whisper,
In the whisper there is a world,
Within that world there is Exuma Infinite;

It stitches itself into the scenery,
The brown windswept oaks,
The lush jungle greenery,
Thriving in a spiritual atmosphere,
Packed just within the humid air,
Threaded into the space and time of life,
A turquoise landscape salty and sheer,
Weaves itself into these mossy oaks of Georgia,
With majestic pervious power,
Dimensions incorporated into each other,
A tapestry resounds in choice,
Two worlds at once,
Intersect underneath the water tower,
Rejoice!
Rejoice!
Rejoice!

"Staring At The Moon Over The Ocean"

Two pelicans after midnight;

The moon now a scarlet fractured lantern swooning,
Refracting silver blades blooming above the sea,
Sitting here as the coastal wind vibrates as it blows,
Just you and me;

One in spirit and one in human clothes,
Searching for Loggerhead angels,
That could be inches in the darkness from my nose,
When two pelicans after midnight,
Came gliding by so suddenly,
So silently,
Confidently,
Without a noise as they cut through the steam,
Silhouetted by the brilliant moon,
And floating off into our dream,
They reminded me that presence,
Is the foundational piece,
Upon which all connection comes.

"(When The Wind Is Not Just) The Wind"

Wind it weave down every path through the trees,
Sometimes largely,
Sometimes very small,
A hurricane,
A crawl,
Why would the weather paint this contradictory scene,
Blustery and stagnant,
Like different parts of me;

Wind it come to wipe away the wrong,
A lullaby,
A very sacred psalm,
A diatribe,
A song,
Why would the weather come to be,
Lovelier than any man could ever dream;

Wind it seems a sentient being,
Compassionate,
And lacking self esteem,
Subdued in the rain,
Or pushing heavy steam,
My, what a world, this world I would flee,
Without the wind to wrap me…

…In its holy filigree.

"Wind Talking"

The wind with its whimsical voice,
Hear the loving voice of God,
Who imparts His words into that of an angel,
Who transfers the message as the words unfold,
Its wisdom breath, extol enchantment,
And listen to enlighten the soul's enhancement,
While the breeze, this messenger…

…Speaks in guiding tones.

"Daddy, I am so grateful! Thank you for our time together. Thank you for believing. Actually, it was never a risk that you wouldn't believe. I know my Daddy and you would never fail to find yourself by my side. In the duality, all we do not get to do together physically can be counterbalanced by what we do spiritually, and that happens because you show up! God is pleased. This is His message to you. Love knows no severance, no break. He intends the eternity of now, and in this now, I am searching for turtles with my father. How amazing is that? Love you, Daddy, so much!"

"The Sandy Flesh Of Exuma"

Rippling waves, an apex array,
Of sun sparkling rain in diamond five dimension shapes,
And this water deep breathes electric light,
Turquoise and opal rainbow white,
And glistens and glitters and pulsates,
Breath after breath inculcate,
Its fabric stretches as it teaches,
And listens, enhances and reaches,
Onto the sandy flesh of Exuma,
Grounds familiar to our holy saints,
Who lay wreathes of prayer on the beaches…

…For us…

…Along this sacred seascape,
As we walk along this pearly dusted space,
And leave our footprints pressed into its face,
The psalms they rise and pirouette in this place,
Dancing for our Lord,
On the sandy flesh of Exuma,
On the sandy banks of its shores.

"Belief"

Belief is found without need for any sound,
When nothing more static can cling to me,
And ridge of doubt and bridge of faith,
Wrestle angels for the arch in my feet;

And so I forward fall and fearless cry,
And never is the fall defeat,
For I am crawling toward the light,
On bloody palms and bleeding knees;

Never consumed in the void of fear,
Never fully unnerved and well replete,
For here I am at the edge of this physical world,
Without a sound,
Not even a whisper,
And what right here is found…

…Is utter, shear belief.

"Water Rainbow Flowers"

Paper thin pastel petals a bouquet,
They in the wind wayward sway,
These water rainbow flowers,
Rounded into a crescent moon arranged,
Held in my humanity,
Yet trimmed in the purity of my soul,
Are threads of organic and ethereal light,
Cusped in the cage of my painfully swollen palm,
Hand-picked from the ranging green fields of my spirit,
In the glassy Exuma Infinite tidal wake,
Where the lush ocean valleys like vibrating harp strings sing,
And the sunrise and sunset interlink;

It is in this atmosphere that I hold you,
The Promised Land here unfolds,
Like a bouquet of water rainbow flowers,
Trimmed from the light of my soul.

"You Are The Exuma Sunrise"

We are basking in the perfect temperature of love,
What will be of us is what is of us and what was of us,
Basking in this perfect climate,
Of faith, of hope, of love, of trust;

Hold my hand in your hand on my heart,
I see the sunrise of your long flowing golden hair,
Pull me into the turquoise blue of your warm ocean eyes,
Sit with me while I tremble into calm,
As I tremble into calm,
And I tremble into calm,
Becoming your obedient pupil,
In this sacred space where we intend to belong,
With your hand on my heart,
And your palm in my palm,
I gaze into Exuma sunrise,
And its infinite reach,
I gaze into Exuma sunrise,
And its infinite white sandy beach…

…As deep and wide as the universe is long.

"A Journey Through Star Fields"

Down a blazing golden road aligned with love and hope,
Sided with emotional guardrails of trust and continuous growth,
Amber glowing sentries spark attention in the night,
And illuminate our bodies,
Like lanterns emitting holy haloed light,
And so we find our way as we always find our way,
Together through the fields of stars,
On the enigmatic journey,
Of eternal life…

…There are tracks of mighty Loggerheads at our feet,
A false crawl bitter tolled,
She has fulfilled the cycle of the harbinger of hope,
And we have just missed this miracle,
There are others that remain hidden in the waters,
Or in the faded blackness of the miles still to go.

"Our Concurrent and Concentric Lives"

You are with me all day long,
And simultaneously you are walking on our spiritual beach,
You are busied,
Happily,
Frenetically,
Running around Exuma Infinite,
Building our family home,
Placing planks of sunlight,
Across beams of purple sky,
And tethered and tied with turquoise waters,
Like a billion stars on opal sparkling walls,
Radiate in blinding diamonds,
On our prominent, white sandy hill,
Overlooking the Mighty Atlantic,
And the shores of Heaven,
Island 366 in the Exuma chain…

…You are laughing in your antics,
Knowing how much work there is to complete,
Before physical death has left me deceased,
And guarding me daily until that release,
Leaving me little messages and cards and riddles and messages,
Daily…

…A streak of turquoise waters in the brown coastal waters,
Washes over my feet.

"Glory"

i.   Conversations On Glory Beach

If dewdrops were moons in the wetlands breeze,
And salt were stars in the seas,
I would breathe liquid light,
And our spirits, they spark,
As doubt disembarks,
As I listen to the phantom curves and contours of the night…

…These are the coils of silver filigree,
The webbing that foams in cresting waves,
Crashing onto Glory Beach,
Yet it is not itself these cresting waves,
But what dwells within each,
For here resonates your brilliant voice,
To guide your father's feet,
Here resonates your laughter and light,
Each time the ocean speaks;

ii.   A Brighter Glow Together

Blending like sheets,
Of wind and zephyr and breath and of breeze,
Revealed, reveled, relished and released,
Behold this mighty, mighty sea;

And the blessed ornamental tapestry,
Each their own color,
A billion sea shells speak,
Threaded in holy mystery,
Where light and light,
Soul and soul,
Are intertwined and weaved;

And so we live,
And live faithfully,
And so we elevate,
In this fidelity,
And so we together brighter glow,
For we are the return on the investment of belief,
For we, simply, believe;

    iii.   *Intentional Ocean*

A servant she seems of the sea,
Pure in confidence and humbled with loyalty,
Whisper wraps ears with its salty steam,
For others the folly, the fancy, the fiction of daydreams,
But for those with elevation,
In a higher vibration,
Hear her voice in the soft curl of the waves…

…As she sacredly speaks.

"Heaven doesn't take me further away from my family. Heaven brings me closer to my family. I am right here. Heaven is right here. It is all one. Tell them that, Daddy. And tell them I said so."

"Our Beads"

i.   *A Constant Gifting*

Crushed Exuma sea shells sparkle in our beads,
Pliably smoothed by her hands into liquid light,
And gently and intently,
Tucked with care into this cord of love,
That she gifts to me in each morning light,
To wear around my neck for the day,
Blending her gift to me with mine to her,
As I crush the hours of the day with my hands,
Sometimes ferociously through grief,
Into liquid light, though limited am I,
To present to her at the end of each day,
My gift of my life in our beads…

…Valued in how I act and think and speak;

ii.   *Necklace Of My Soul's Light*

Show them, all those angels worthy of your space,
All of the elevated souls of which you choose to grace,
Show them the beads your father gifts you daily,
Show them the love we share,
Show them the unbreakable cord of light,
Show them my faith and show them my fear,
Show them the gift that is worthy of our love,
This necklace of my soul's light that you wear,
Show them my courage and show them my despair,
And my hours and hours and hours of prayer,
Show them all worthy of your space,
This necklace of my soul's light that you wear.

"A Great Father"

The velvet arid flakes like hot summer snow fell from trees,
And swirled down the echo chambers of night washed beach,
Listlessly aloofly floating,
Where on earth to go,
Where on earth to go;

And the breeze that carried leaves to the sea,
Is the very same wind that inland sings,
Beauty has its juxtaposing,
Just as the shadows lurk into the glow…

…Thunder scathing rain it coats the dream,
Heavy showers rumble distantly,
Rash of lightning scar the shepherd's scene,
As He tends His herd sleeping dryly and quietly,
Always eyes affixed to flanking sounds,
Always with an ear to vibrations on the ground,
For in faith though fear may find you fully,
He will rage against the misery…

…And draw you near.

"Divinity's Bloom"

Star shadows crawl like bronzed filigree,
Delicately ornate in the flesh of the clouds,
That pulse in the lightning over the sea…

…And to think that once we spent our time linked to worry,
What is it we are running toward,
And with this stress,
What is the hurry;

Star fields spread in the glossy haze of nebula,
Just beyond our eyes,
Yet they are there shining in the darkness,
They are alive…

…And you know the crime is in the fear,
For the fear it fails us in its fury,
What is it we are flailing toward,
In the spent canisters of fuel and worry;

Rest in these veins where a slower breath prevails,
And star shadows merge in the brightest mist of moon,
And we find that all along,
The shadows are just ribs on the vibrant petals,
Of divinity's flowering bloom.

"For Momma"

i.   Galaxy Within Galaxy

Collecting diamond rains in radiant palms,
Exuma diamas regn,
Glowing through the opal liquid currents,
Cupped in hands,
Like galaxies within galaxies,
A mother and a child sharing cellular strands,
Blooming light in its purest form,
Of one body that births into two brands,
That resonate in the heart;

Spirit ambles intently in amber tinted aqua minted fog,
Within a heavy cloud bank drifting along,
Piercing the heavens with her infectious laughter
Shining through,
Singing her lunar blood song;

Aligned in perfect adhesion,
Devout to purposeful meaning and reason,
She smiles and radiates,
On her special day,
Singing her lunar blood song;

ii.   Momma

Momma, your womb like a nebula star nursery,
It my home within your flesh,
Momma, your lunar blood is in my veins,
Your solar skin and mine like interwoven mesh,
Momma, your moon is the moon most sacred,
For in you I cradle,
My soul in yours nests.

"This Current Life Box"

This family of four;

As water afire in liquid electricity,
Radiant in sparkling water light,
Diamond crystals streamed in felicity,
A dream to dream to conquer this life;

Until the fourth has fully entertained this fight,
Until the fourth of us crosses into the light,
This current life box continues to unfold,
And so in spirit we continue to grow old;

When that day come, as water afire speaks,
When all four of us walk the infinite beach,
When the reset comes to start us all again,
We will be what we always are,
A family of four, current life box and life box,
With always a cycle,
And never an end.

"Washing Feet"

i.   Lonely Is The Flesh

The washing of the feet,
And the washing of the hands,
The washing gives release,
To the washing of the man,
For the waters speak and breathe,
And the waters understand,
That the water bring release,
For the loneliness of man;

ii.   Impactfully Impossible

An inventory of angel deeds is not easy to toll,
An inventory of miracles no bucket for starfish holds,
An inventory of contact like stones frame this sturdy road,
An inventory of union between two dedicated souls…

…Is, to the truth of its magnitude…

…Impactfully impossible,
But in the washing of the feet,
The vision will enhance,
For in the washing of the feet,
Comes the holiness of man.

"Through The Blooms Of Spirit Night"

Spent the wind, it howled vacant,
Barring eclipsing pirouetted lightning,
Distant storms of distortion and discomfort,
Thunder crash ignites misplacement,
Merge with rash that comes enlightening,
Mesmerizing the dissipating humid cloaks,
The air itself a swamp of oxygen soaked,
To the bone and to its limit,
Though darkness prevails,
It is only approximate,
To the brilliance and radiance that emerges,
In the cooled wake of the storm,
That the clear sky wipes and purges,
Releasing into the night a soul dance,
As the moon rises from God's own hands…

…Lift our eyes to star fields…

…Now that the threat is slight…

…And embrace the strengthening awakened walk…

…Through the blooms of spirit night.

"Space Weather"

Celestial seasons curled into a blustering nebula,
Star fields ignite in the mystic, snaking, swirling winds,
Shaping emerald clouds and gassy sparkling shores,
Where diamonds rain in spectacular parades,
Of glistening soft glass and rainbows one thousand miles thick,
The space weather is the mixing of everything,
Collapsed in time,
Exuma turquoise colors wash down the sands,
Of Jekyll Island and its driftwood spine,
Flowing across bushels of Adam's Needle,
Where the Small-Leaf Arrowhead plies,
And the Aster and Palmetto Palms ring the oaks,
Now deep in the Exuma Infinite soak,
Of heavenly waters that blend into one,
Mesh the physical world in which we find,
The dimensions are one organism,
That breathe no space nor time,
The dimensions are one organism,
Breathe no space nor time.

"An Angel's Shore"

Pelicans tucked into quiet bundles on stubby wooden posts,
Salt, its scent it vents its voice in the silence of this coast,
Bobcats are perched in the tallest trees,
Peering with such pinnacle vision,
Their eyes like amber stars in the deep night,
Twinkle in the canopies,
In such subtle ways that no human eye may see,
But for the glowing crescent tongue,
Of a wagging summer moon,
The darkness would be a forest itself,
Of interlinking blackened trees,
Yet there are shadows and if there are shadows,
Then there must be light…

…Here are the footprints of Heaven left upon this angel's
shore…

…Glistening moon swept white.

"Immortal Water Light"

We are water,
We are of light,
Stars composed of water,
We are of liquid life,
We are the horizon,
The bright streams before the dusk,
We are time and space,
Within each one of us,
For we, we are of water,
And therefore we are life,
We the cells of breathing water,
Immortal water light.

"Another Planet"

Earthly walkers, your blinking lights red and bold,
Traverse sand plains, in search of tracks of sacred soul,
Miles away they glow in the darkness like bright cherry suns,
Miles away they creep closer and closer as the minutes run,
Miles away they may as well be on another planet,
For deep down the desolate south end of this beach…

…Is itself…

…Another planet.

"Eyes To The Heavens"

The galaxy flows - an ocean of liquid light,
A beating, pumping resilient celestial heart,
Pulsing to the silent darkness of night,
And imbedding salty sand in our scars,
While in our pursuit of eternal life,
As we are fleshed in the skins of stars,
Though never more are we akin,
To these fiery satellites burning bright,
If we turn our eyes from the sky,
For in the mystic fabric of a blackened night,
We find out exactly who and what we are,
As we turn our eyes to the heavens,
As we turn our eyes to the within,
And within we find these heavens,
Are Heaven's prints within.

"LTT9779b"

Pure poetry two hundred sixty two light-years from Earth,
Cascading in fiery surface, ash and flaming dirt,
The scorching exoplanet, a toxic iconic world,
Casting reflective clouds, silicate in swirls;

Light crashes into it like mirror,
And shines brighter than the sun,
With metals as harsh as titanium,
That spew out from engine in fire tongues;

Its halo a maze of reflective metal clouds,
That percolate and bubble and gurgle glassy shrouds,
That blanket the atmosphere in a poison all its own,
Raining silver sheets of splintered metal stones;

Though there is beauty encapsulated in its heart,
The high shine highly reflective of its hosting star,
Its majestic albedo glimmers a quantity of light,
Rarely seen in any galaxy on any given night;

So is Saturn's Enceladus,
So is Jupiter's Europa,
Sing brightly like this burning world,
But nothing seems as hot as its surface,
Baked from the star around which it closely curls,
For nothing is quite like this planet…

…Except the grief that erupts from my soul…

…For my precious girl.

"Colony of Messengers"

Suddenly, in a massive orchestration,
A colony of fireflies in the canopies sing with light,
Thousands of messengers illuminate in spiraling flight,
Calling for others in gowns like glowing sprites,
Of green, and scarlet and orange and opal white,
That swoop collectively toward me in a liquid stream;

they land upon the fallen oak,
they radiate this scene,
they illuminate the fallen spokes,
of the trunks of mighty jungle beach trees,
they crawl upon the dry sand,
like glowing carpet at my feet,
and create the perfect atmosphere,
awakened to this beach.

*"Daddy, a little further, I promise. I know the darkness obscures
your view, but trust me. Daddy! Over here! Come on! Over there,
near the smooth fallen oak where we set up our hammock during
the day. I promise. Keep going further south like one hundred
yards."*

"Agape (Merging Dimensions)"

And, without a sound, in a sacred silence,
Agape;

A flowing heavy bank of mystic fog of delicate lights,
Emerges from the flesh of the night,
Already present, hidden only from hindered eyes,
Already present, for those who dare the kingdom of sight,
Behold,
A thousand strings of electric blues and aqua greens,
Sparkle through smoky convergence,
Like a million cans of paint thrown against the wind,
Spreading and splashing like rivers of smeared color,
Crawling the wind, its lively canvas,
Swirled together in these waters, this air, this space,
Baroque temples bricked in biblical liquid gold,
Form rivers of dimensions merging these two scenes,
Aqua opal salt crisply scents the glistening air,
Reflecting off of transparent clear waters,
Pastel jade and emerald green strings of lighter currents,
Give way to white sea foam minty hues,
Vibrancy and brilliance,
Are ours, Kayleigh,
Anam Chara,
Blend and mesh and enrich and consume;

Mossy silver trees waiver in the august breeze,
Celeste tranquil sky-blue smoke, brown blur,
It, tinge the tropical heat in oceanic greens,
And dark turquoise in mysterious sheen,
It speaks of the promising depths of mysteries,
Without revealing its secrets,
Turquoise blue, the caretaker of serenity,
Beauty, to soothe the tides of an anxious soul;

Lanterns of lavender white turquoise sweats,
Like opal rain, an angel's prayer,
Radiating warmth in calming appeal,
An inviting environment strikes out against all doubt,
For here is the house of the Lord;

Energizing aqua shimmering with enchantment,
Pastel shades speak of hidden wisdom coins and pearls,
Adventurous minds are mining,
Where the sand swirls with the broken beige waves,
Copper turquoise bands spread like oil in the branches,
Warm and cool tones, rusty orange-brown subdued undertones,
Cyan whispery, deep sky and cobalt blue,
Splashing in the midnight heavenly iridescence,
Dancing between sapphires and emeralds in ethereal splendor,
Neon turquoise flash, electric voice, lightning,
The intensity it sheds in the enlivening personality,
Of this majestic stage;

Sea foam, lush, bubbling, floats through star gardens,
Like flakes of human skin and human years,
Shadows, human doubts, hints of gray undertones,
Vibrantly evoke innocence in the presence of this angel,
We stand here together,
Both of us grounded and royal;

In the washing of the sea spray, sea salted air,
Within the rustling of tropical plants,
Swaying gently in the heavy heat of coastal breezes,
Turquoise chalky dust gathers like sea shell sand at my feet,
An intense light explodes,
No black shadows beneath the lighter hues may endure,
Standing here in the fullness of her body of light,
I finally, with such perfect vision, can see,
My daughter standing here,
My daughter standing here.

"Turtle Lightning"

Life itself lives in the laughter of this light,
Lightning sizzles and crackles grappling through cloud fields,
Dancing decadently to the ocean's delight,
Whistling with emerald beads wrapped in Rosary white,
Radiate a blackened ashy humid, heated night,
Illuminating a turtle in the dune line digging,
Flash across the ocean in opal confetti flight,
That explode into tributaries,
And branch off into the darkness,
Beneath the gatherers of Holy sprites,
Through which fluorescence glows;

She, this Loggerhead,
She, an ancient wisdom, understands,
She takes our audience,
As she lay quietly in the sand,
She blinks her eyes in the moonlight,
As she releases her eggs into this land,
And thanks us for our presence,
Our persistence,
Our protection under the circumstance,
Knowing that if we could,
We would cradle her in our hands.

"We have walked for six hours, seven maybe! Daddy! Daddy! I told you we would find her! Look at her pitting. Let's just sit here a while and watch her quietly. We are a part of this, Daddy, because you are here. Remember I always tell you, I can go to Jekyll Island whenever I want, but I can't go with my Daddy, if my Daddy doesn't come to Jekyll Island. Thank you for listening to me, for coming here, for walking with me, for elevating with me. For being my Daddy. For helping me with these miracles. For us. Love you!"